OXFORD

Cool

Course Book

3

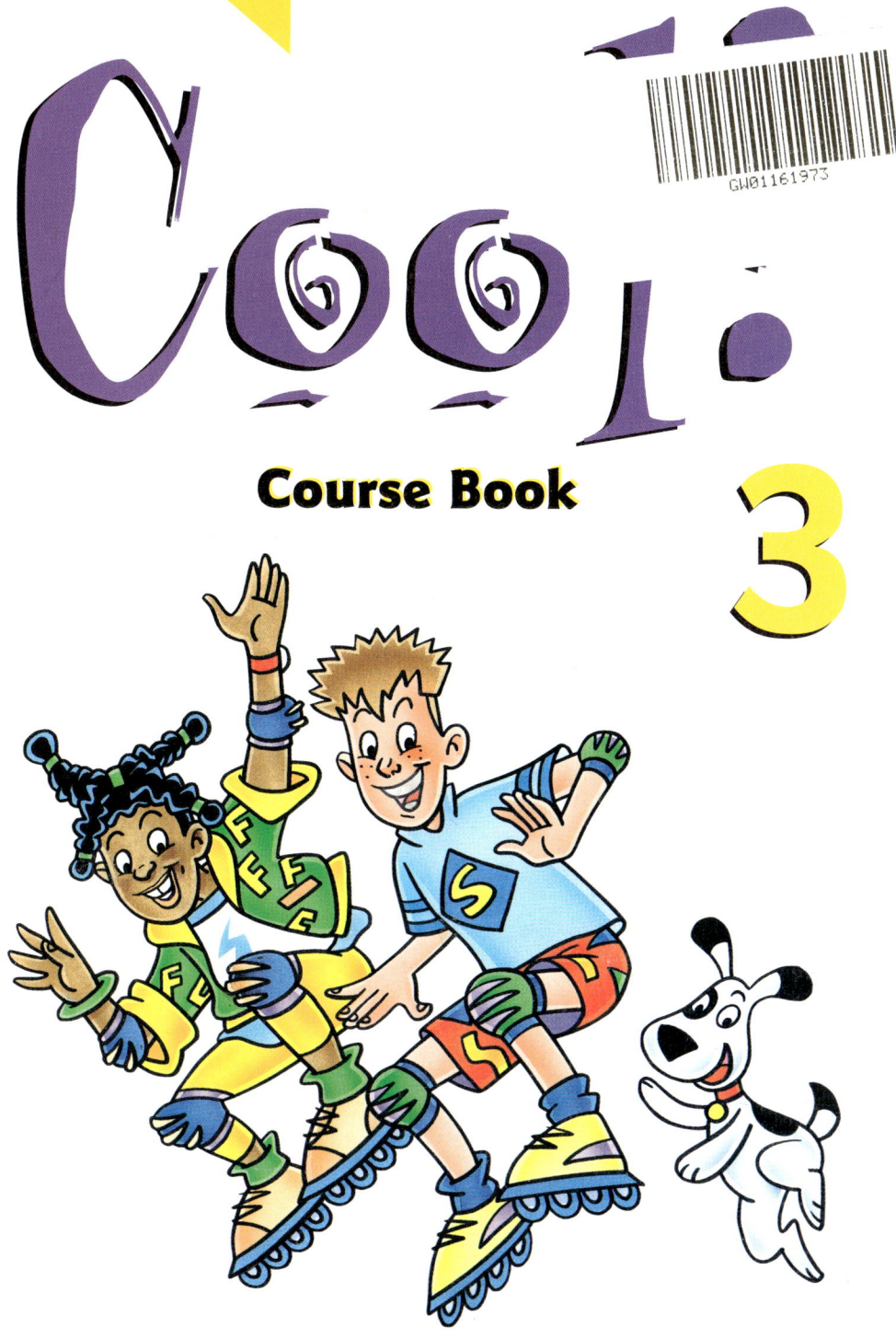

Jackie Holderness
Wendy Superfine
Stella Maidment

2 In the Playground!

 **Listen and write the numbers.**

- ② clapping
- ⑨ drinking
- ④ running
- ① playing football
- ⑤ climbing
- ③ reading
- ⑦ singing
- ⑧ writing
- ⑥ eating
- ⑩ sleeping

 **Read and find.**

1 How many children are there in the playground?
2 Find 4 things beginning with 'b'.
3 Find 5 red things.
4 Who is eating an apple?
5 Find 3 things you use in the classroom.
6 How many children are playing football?
7 What can you see under the tree?
8 How many children are wearing a hat?
9 What's behind Mr Crumble?

page 80

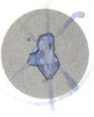  **Listen and number.**

 **Now read and match.**

Can I have my ball, please?   It's a ghost story!
Do you like cheese sandwiches?   In the tree!
What are you reading?   Here you are!
Have you got a pen?   Two o'clock.
Where's my hat?   Yes ... Mmmm delicious.
What time is it?   Yes. What colour?

page 81

1 My Day

 **Listen and write the numbers.**

4 twelve o'clock   1 a quarter to seven

3 half past eleven   2 a quarter past three

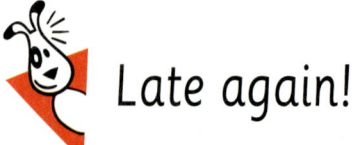

Late again!

**Listen and circle the time you hear.
Draw the time on the clocks.**

1. Robin Hood — (twelve o'clock) / ten o'clock
2. Peter Pan — (half past three) / half past ten
3. Space Adventure... — (twenty past ten) / ten past ten
4. Snow White — a quarter to eleven / (a quarter past eleven)
5. Lost in the Jungle — ten to nine / (ten to one)
6. House of Horror — (twenty to twelve) / twenty to eleven

page 82

8  Let's sing a song.

This is the way I jump out of bed,
Jump out of bed, jump out of bed.
This is the way I jump out of bed,
On a Monday morning.

This is the way
I wash my face, ...

This is the way
I brush my hair, ...

This is the way
I clean my teeth, ...

This is the way
I run to school, ...

This is the way
I stay in bed, ...
On a Sunday morning!

 Look at the pictures. Read and number.
Then draw the times on the clocks.

Picture

3	I do my homework at three o'clock.
6	At a quarter to six I go to bed.
2	At twenty-five to nine I go to school.
5	At a quarter past five I have a bath.
4	At half past four I play with my friends.
1	I get up at half past seven.

10  Listen and write the times. Then ask your friend.

"What time do you get up, Mr Crumble?"

"Oh, I get up at half past seven."

	Mr Crumble's day	My friend's day	My day
1 get up	7.30	6.00 am	6.30 am
2 have a shower	7.45	8.10 pm	7:00 pm
3 have breakfast	8:10	7.30 am	8:00 am
4 go to school	8:30	7.40 am	7.40 am
5 have lunch	12:30	12.00 am	3.50 pm
6 finish school	4.00	11.30 am	12.25 am
7 have tea	5:15	7.50 pm	7.10 pm
8 go to bed	10.00	9.00 pm	9.00 pm

 **Draw and write about your day.**

1. I get up at half past six .

2. Then I have breakfast at seven o'clock .

3. I go to school on foot at 8.00 eight o'clock .

4. I do homework at sixton (six) o'clock .

5. I then have a bath at nineton (seven) o'clock .

6. I go to bed at nine o'clock .

14 Penfriends

3 Hilltop Road
Oxford OX3 5DP
England
THE WORLD

15th September

Dear Ricardo
Hi, I'm Sarah — your new penfriend. I'm ten years old and I live in Oxford. I start school at nine o'clock and finish at half past three. I have lunch at twenty to one.
On Mondays, I have my cello lesson at a quarter to five.
We have dinner at half past seven. I go to bed at half past nine.
Please write soon. Tell me about your day. Bye for now.

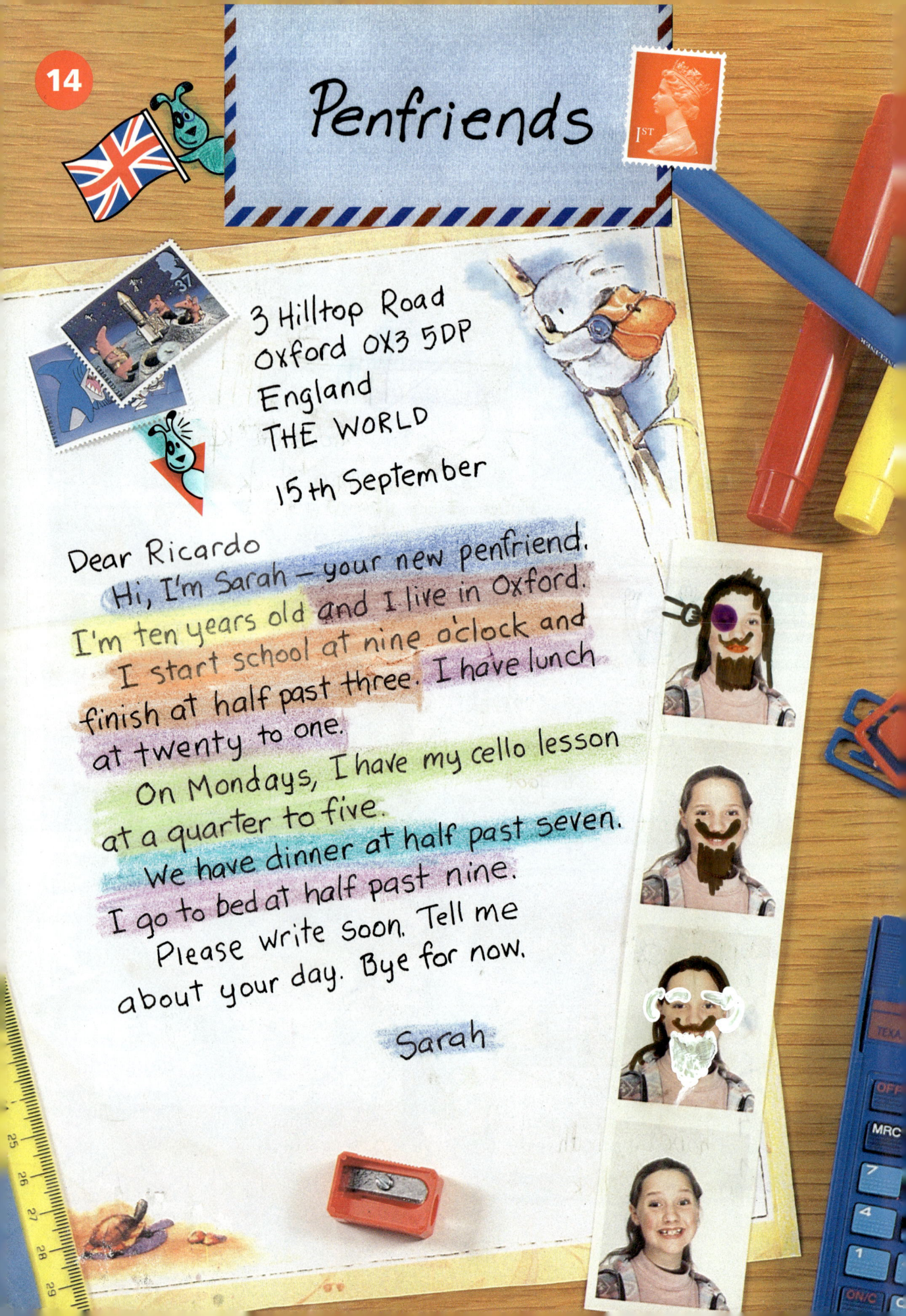

Sarah

16  Read. Then write the sentences.

I get up at twenty past seven.
I go to school at ten past eght.
I have my lunch at half past twelve.
I play football at quarter to five.
I have a bath at half past nine.
I go to bed at ten o'clock.

Difficult ☐ Quite difficult ☐ OK ☐ Quite easy ✓ Easy ☐

2 Free Time Fun

 **Listen and write the numbers.**

5 dance   4 sing   6 play the guitar

1 cook   3 paint   2 play table tennis

# The school band.

 **Listen and put a tick (✓) or a cross (✗).**

		👦	👧
1 play basketball	🏀	✓	✓
2 ski	🎿	✗	✗
3 ride a bike	🚲	✓	✓
4 cook	🍳	✗	✓

Find someone in your class who can ...

1 Play the piano

Name: *Klaudia i Manuela*

2 Ride a horse

Name: *Klaudia*

3 Swim

Name: *Łukasz*

4 Ski

Name: *Damian*

20

Let's sing a song.

I work all week in a bakery,
I put cakes in boxes all day.
I go home in the evenings
and I watch TV.
    And on Friday nights …
    I phone my Auntie May.

But … on Saturdays I get in my car,
I drive to the seaside - it isn't too far.
Then I stand on my surfboard and ride on the waves.
I love Saturdays!

I work all week in an office block,
I sit and look at a computer screen.
I go home in the evenings
and I read a book.
And on Friday nights …
I read a magazine.

But … on Saturdays I get in my car,
I drive to the seaside - it isn't too far.
Then I stand on my surfboard and ride on the waves.
I love Saturdays!

Listen. Then play the game.

Do you play football on Mondays?
Yes.
Do you watch television on Tuesdays?
No.
Do you swim on Saturdays?
Yes.
Are you Tiff?
Yes.

22 Let's play a game.

Can you ...

1. draw an elephant?
2. count to 20 in English?
3. close one eye?
4. name four things beginning with 'p'?
5. say the time in English?
6. name six animals in English?
7. hold your pencil on your finger?
8. sing a *Cool!* song?
9. touch your nose with your tongue?
10. say the alphabet in English?
11. find five blue things?
12. jump like a kangaroo?

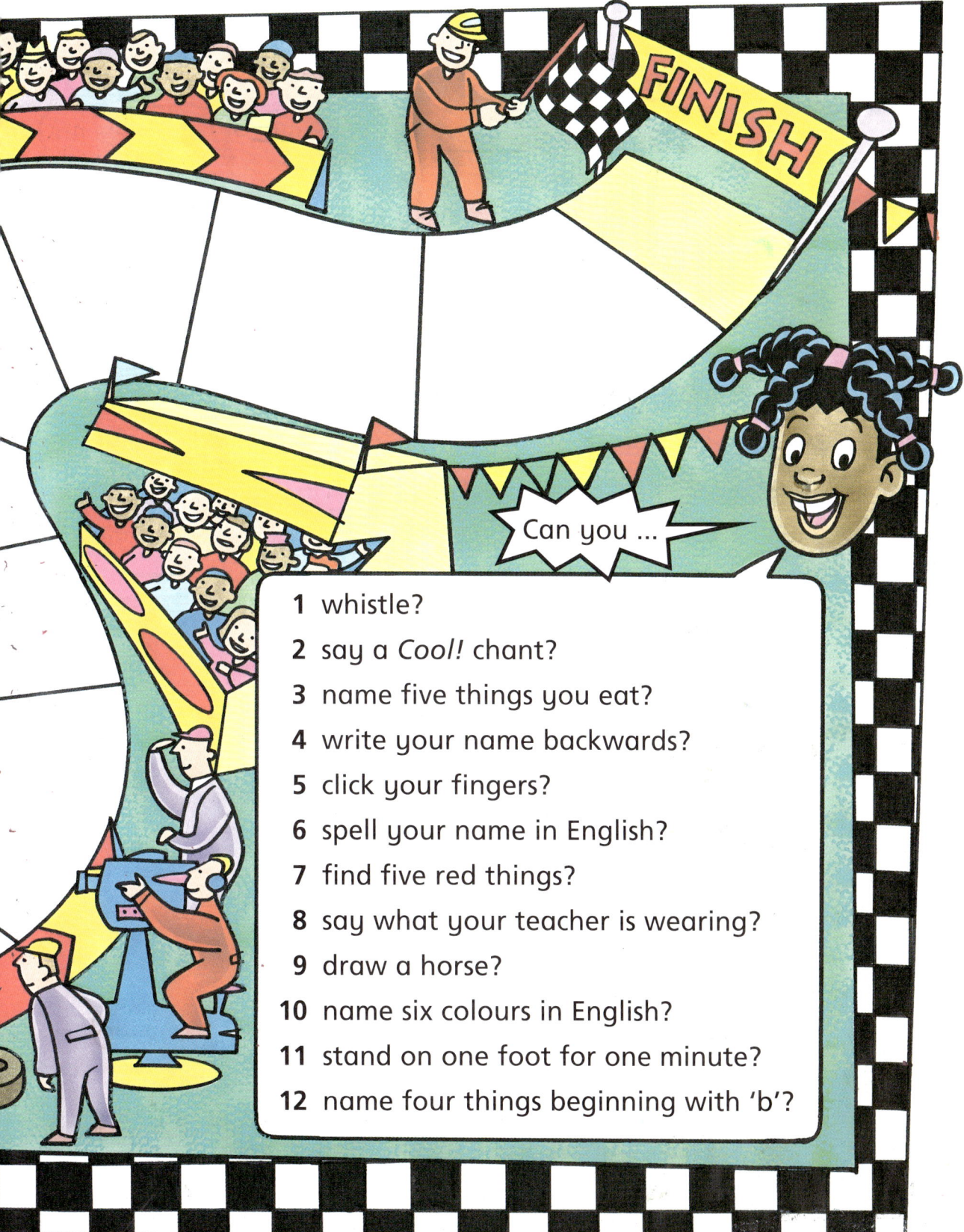

Can you ...

1 whistle?
2 say a *Cool!* chant?
3 name five things you eat?
4 write your name backwards?
5 click your fingers?
6 spell your name in English?
7 find five red things?
8 say what your teacher is wearing?
9 draw a horse?
10 name six colours in English?
11 stand on one foot for one minute?
12 name four things beginning with 'b'?

Penfriends

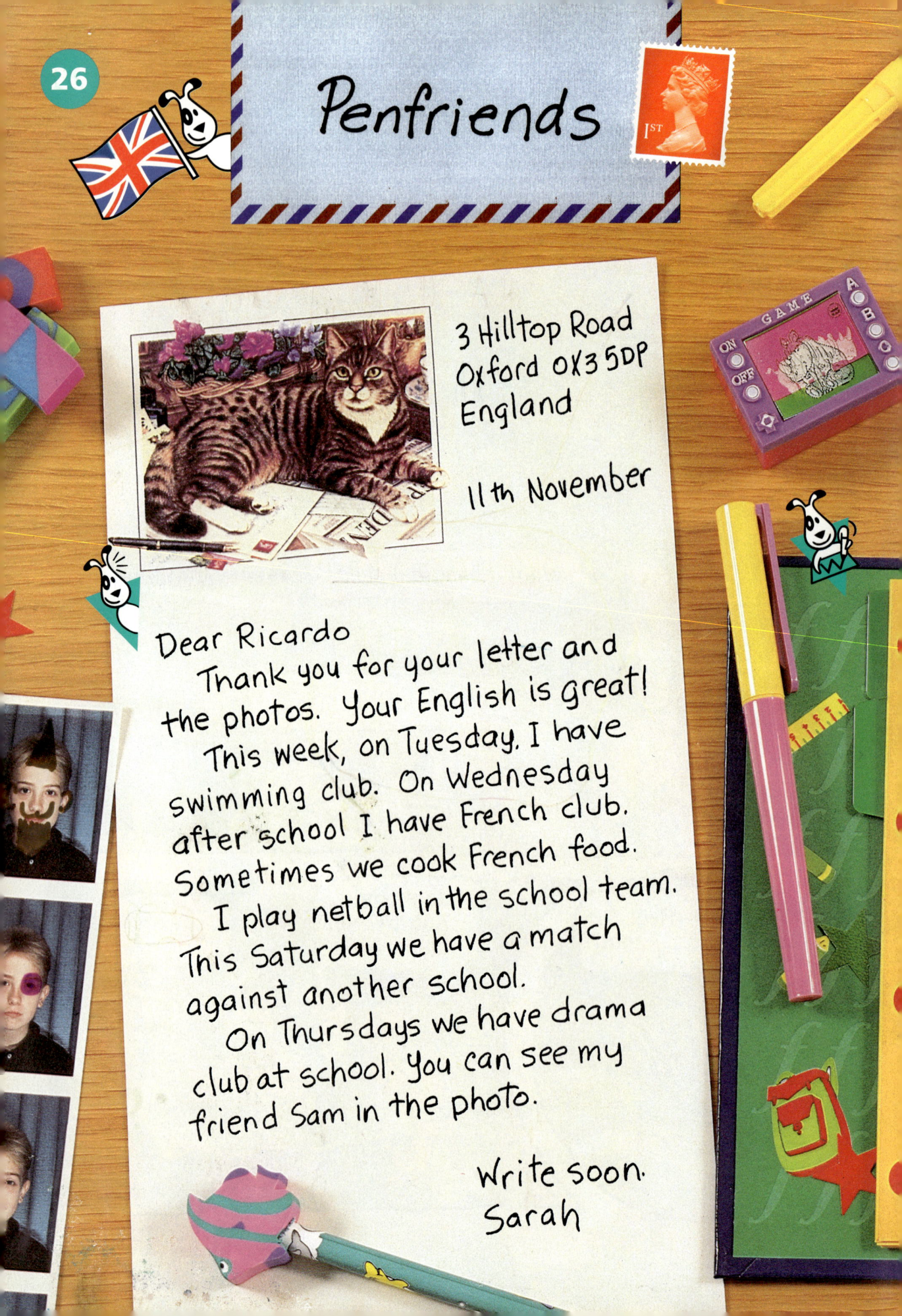

3 Hilltop Road
Oxford OX3 5DP
England

11th November

Dear Ricardo
 Thank you for your letter and the photos. Your English is great!
 This week, on Tuesday, I have swimming club. On Wednesday after school I have French club. Sometimes we cook French food.
 I play netball in the school team. This Saturday we have a match against another school.
 On Thursdays we have drama club at school. You can see my friend Sam in the photo.

Write soon.
Sarah

28

Write the days. Then listen and match.

1 T **H U R S** d a y

2 **M** o **N** d **A Y**

3 **F r i d a** y

4 **S** u **N** d a y

5 **T u e s d** a y

6 **W E** d **N** e **S d a** y

7 s **A T** u **R** d a y

 Difficult ☐    Quite difficult ☐    OK ☐    Quite easy ☐    Easy ☒

3 Special Days

Listen and write the numbers.

① 14th February ② 22nd August

③ 25th December ⑤ 31st March

⑥ 5th November ④ 3rd April

 Write the invitation to Mr Crumble's party. Invite a friend.

Please come to a PARTY!
To: Bartek
Date: 3rd June Time: four o'clock
Address: 9 London Road

From: Flash, Speedi,

 Let's say a chant.

When's your birthday?
I can't remember!
It's on the 1st September!

When's your birthday?
I think it's soon!
It's on the 23rd June!

When's your birthday?
Can you say?
It's the 29th May!

When's your birthday?
Is it in December?
No - the 2nd November!

 Read about a special day.

 Answer these questions about Longwood.

1 What dates is the Safari Park open?
   From 1st February to 31st October

2 What times can you visit Longwood House?
   from 11:30 am t 4:30 pm

3 How much is a go-kart ride? £2.00

4 How much is a train ride? £1.50

5 How much is the maze? free £ free

Listen and tick (✔) the places Flash and Speedy visit.

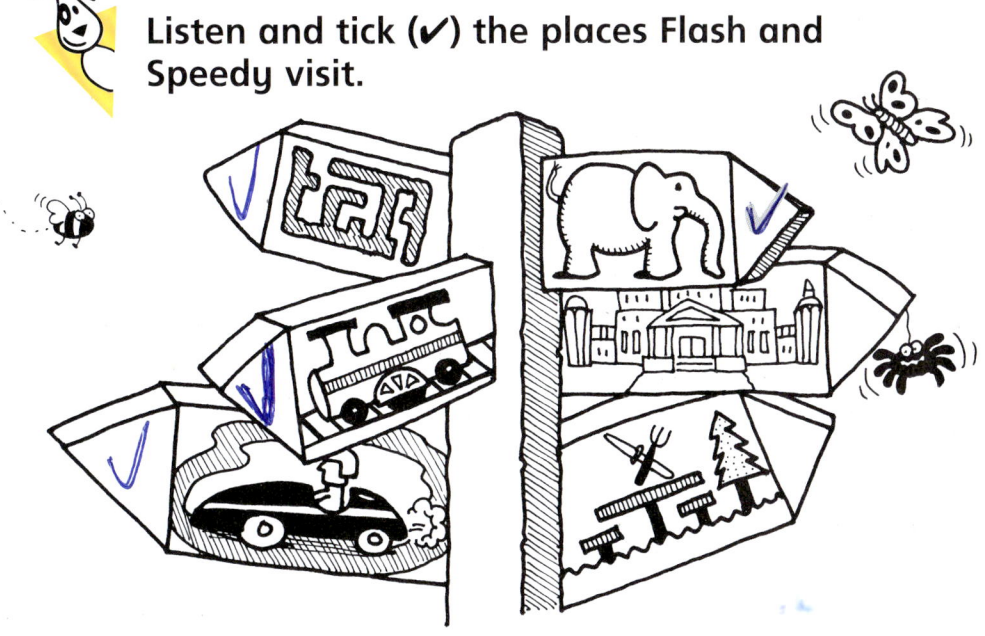

Listen and write the numbers.

- 2 house
- 5 train
- 8 go-kart track
- 6 café
- 4 garden
- 7 souvenir shop
- 3 maze
- 1 safari park

Listen. Then ask and answer about other places in the park.

Excuse me, where's the maze?
It's next to the house.
Thank you.

Draw a line out of the maze.

Now write the directions - turn left, turn right, go straight on.

1 Turn left at the tree.
2 Go straight on at the bench.
3 turn right at the statue.
4 turn right at the bird.

5 turn left at the flowers.
6 Turn left at the fountain.
7 Go straight on at the lion.
8 Turn right at the bin.

EPISODE 3
ESCAPE FROM DIAMOND CAVE

7
Giant strawberries! And bananas!
Mmmm! I love strawberries.
8
Later ...
Another one? Conrad, don't be greedy.
GLOP!
9
Help! A s-s-snake!
Quick! Let's go!
10
Footprints!
There are people here too.
11
Perhaps they can help us.
Let's see. Come on.
GLOP
Continues ...

Penfriends

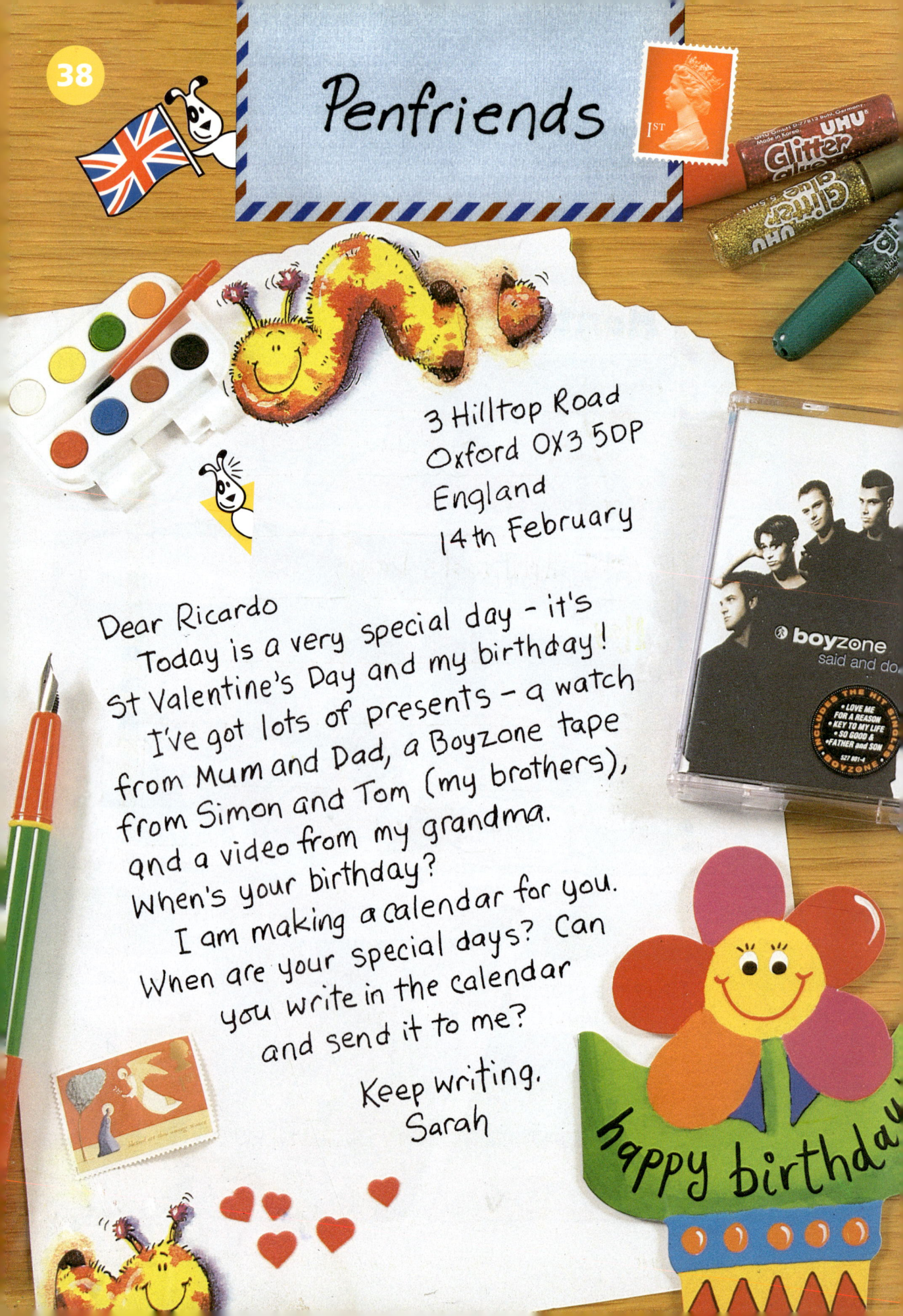

3 Hilltop Road
Oxford OX3 5DP
England
14th February

Dear Ricardo
 Today is a very special day – it's St Valentine's Day and my birthday!
 I've got lots of presents – a watch from Mum and Dad, a Boyzone tape from Simon and Tom (my brothers), and a video from my grandma. When's your birthday?
 I am making a calendar for you. When are your special days? Can you write in the calendar and send it to me?

Keep writing,
Sarah

Month	Me	You
January		New Year's day
February	♥ My birthday!	St Valentine's d
March		
April	April Fool's Day	My birthday Easter
May		
June		
July		
August	Carnival Time	
September		
October		Halloween
November	Bonfire night	
December		Christmas

40

Listen and circle the dates you hear.
Then listen again and match.

Difficult ☐   Quite difficult ☐   OK ☑   Quite easy ☑   Easy ☑

4 Famous People

Listen and write the numbers.

(1) singer (5) dancer (3) athlete

(6) footballer (4) detective ( ) actor

Supermarket Stars

1． Look, Speedy. There's Lorna Love!
Who's Lorna Love?

2． She's an actress. She's on TV in 'Dear Friends'!
Oh, yes - your favourite programme.

4． Is she wearing a blue coat?
Yes!

5． There she is - next to the bananas.

7． There she is - next to the biscuits!
What's she doing there?

8． I'm Lorna Love ... and I love Baker's Biscuits!
Thanks, Lorna.

3

Is she short with fair hair?

No, she's tall with dark hair!

6

No! That's a man. He's got a beard!

9 Later ...

Look, Speedy! That's you and me! We're TV stars!

I'm Lorna Love ... and I love Baker's Biscuits!

Look. Then draw your own pictures. Use these words: tall, short, curly, straight.

TALL

SHORT

STRAIGHT

44 Look at the picture and write *Yes* or *No*.

	Jamie	Benny	Robbie
Is he tall?	Yes	Yes	No
Has he got a beard?	No	Yes	No
Is he fair?	No	Yes	Yes
Has he got glasses?	No	Yes	Yes
Has he got curly hair?	Yes	Yes	No
Is he dark?	Yes	No	No
Has he got straight hair?	No	No	Yes
Has he got a moustache?	Yes	Yes	No
Is he short?	No	No	Yes

page 88

Listen. Then play the game.

46 Read. Then complete the chart.

Mimi

① Mimi is an actress. She is very beautiful! She's French and she lives in Paris with her cat, Fifi. Mimi's favourite food is snails.

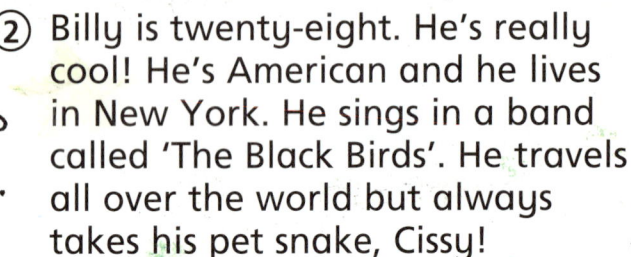

② Billy is twenty-eight. He's really cool! He's American and he lives in New York. He sings in a band called 'The Black Birds'. He travels all over the world but always takes his pet snake, Cissy!

Billy

Fiona

③ Fiona is Scottish and lives in Edinburgh. She's nineteen. She's a wonderful athlete. Her favourite food is bananas. She's great!

Name	Mimi	Billi	Fiona
Age	I don't know	28	19
Nationality	FRENCH	American	Scottish
Lives in	PARIS	NEW YORK	Edinburgh
Job	actors	SINGER	athlete
Favourite food	snails	I don't know	bananas

page 89

Let's sing a song.

I'm Daniel Defarr,
I'm a famous film star,
I'm handsome and I'm never shy.
When I walk down the street,
The people I meet,
Say, 'What an incredible guy!'

I'm Daniel Defarr,
I drive a fast car,
And I always have a sun tan.
When I drive anywhere,
The people all stare,
And say, 'What an interesting man!'

I'm Daniel Defarr,
I'm a famous film star,
I always wear orange and yellow.
And wherever I go,
The people say, 'Oh!
What a sensational fellow!'

48
EPISODE 4
ESCAPE FROM DIAMOND CAVE

1.
Where are we now?
I don't know.
It's hot here.

2.
Listen! I can hear voices.
Yes, look over there!

3.
Poor things. They are very tired.
Perhaps we can help them to escape.
How?

4.

5.
It's too hot, Eva. Can they stop?
No! They can't stop. I know there are more diamonds here.

6.
I've got an idea.
What?

7
Come on. Follow me!
8
We need three more strawberries.
Watch out for snakes.
9
A few minutes later …
Ready? OK, one, two …
10
… three!
Hey! What's happening?
I can't see!
11
Hooray! They're escaping!
munch!
munch!
WOW!

Continues …

Penfriends

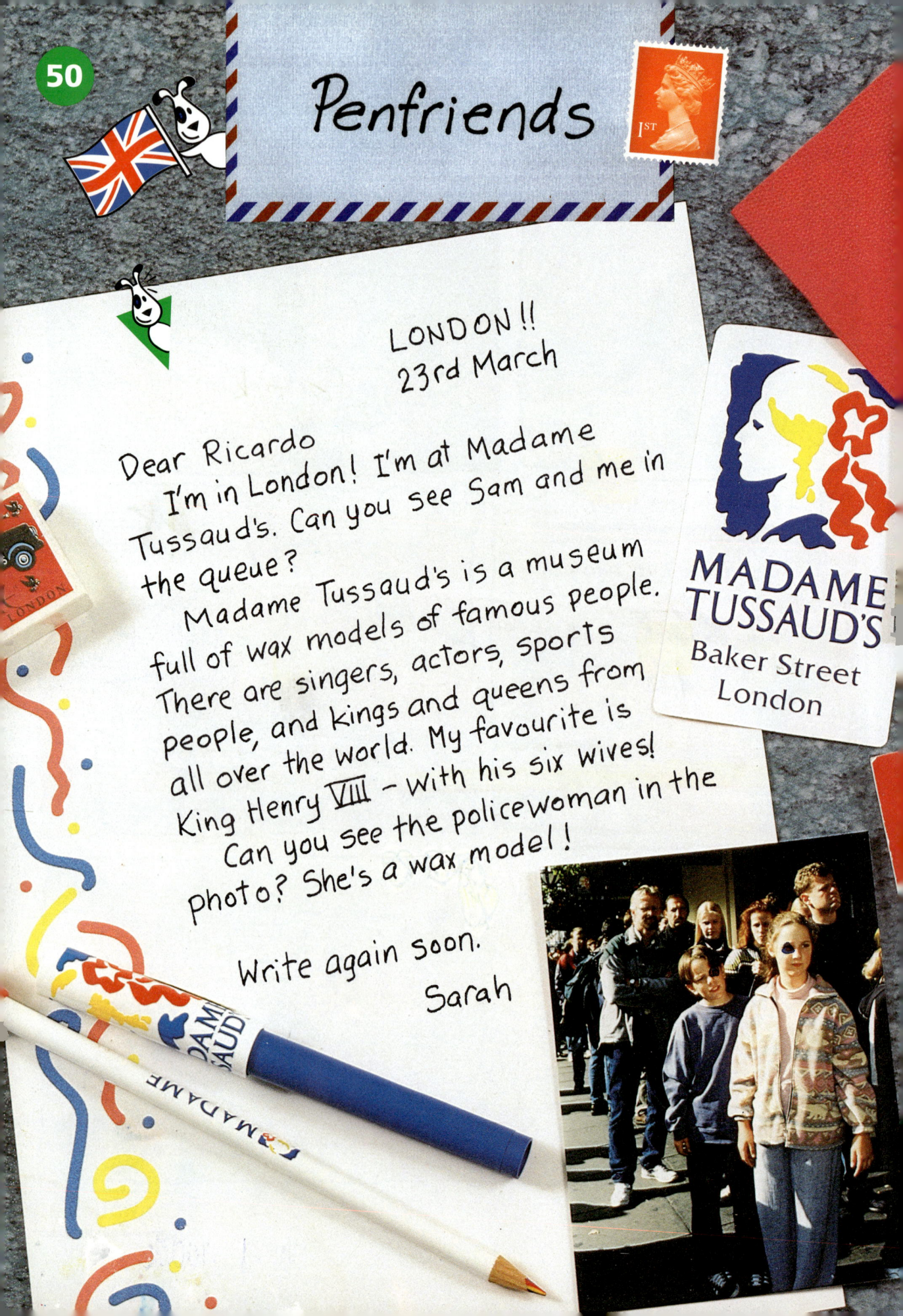

LONDON!!
23rd March

Dear Ricardo

I'm in London! I'm at Madame Tussaud's. Can you see Sam and me in the queue?

Madame Tussaud's is a museum full of wax models of famous people. There are singers, actors, sports people, and kings and queens from all over the world. My favourite is King Henry VIII - with his six wives! Can you see the policewoman in the photo? She's a wax model!

Write again soon.
Sarah

MADAME TUSSAUD'S
Baker Street
London

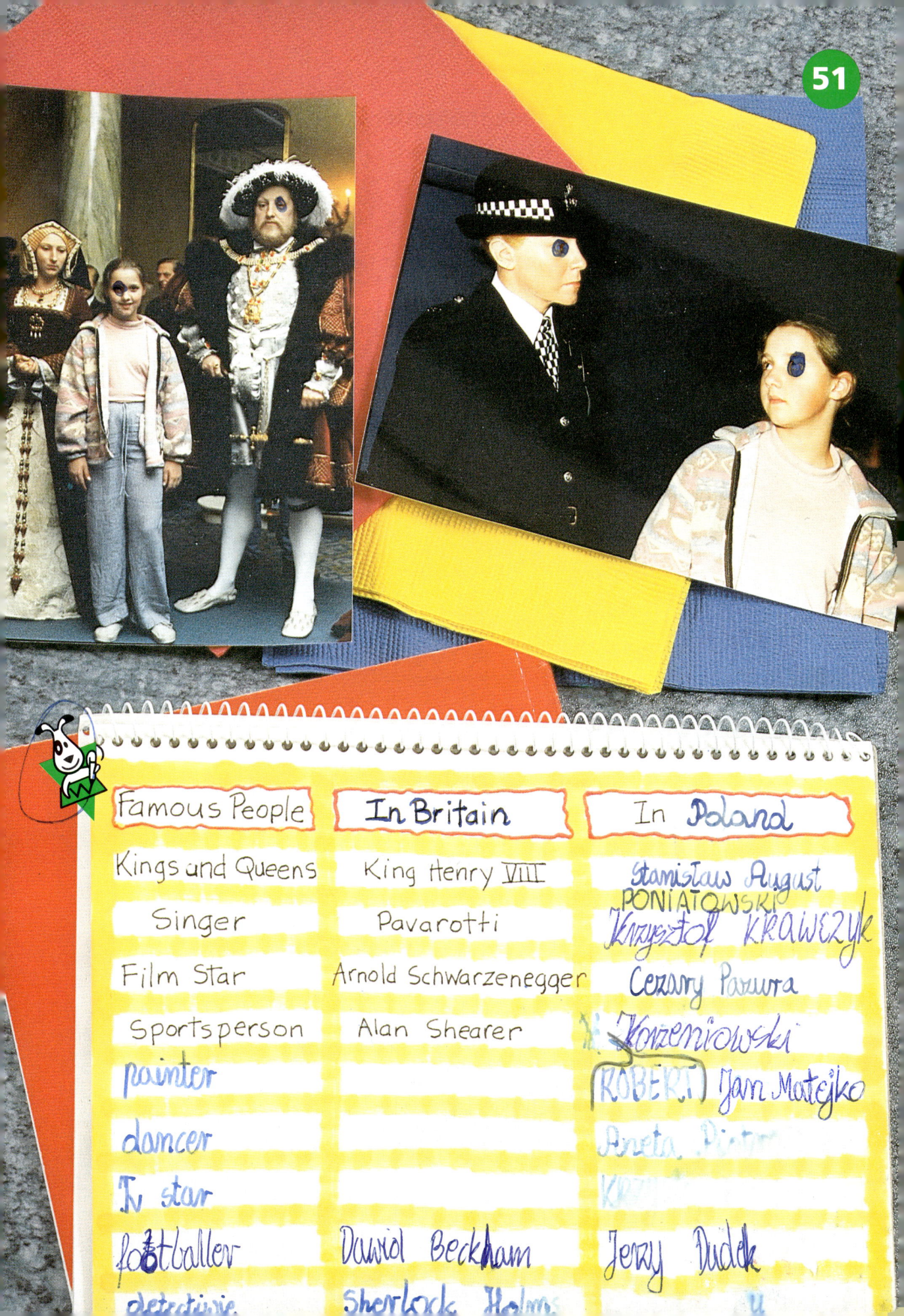

Famous People	In Britain	In Poland
Kings and Queens	King Henry VIII	Stanisław August PONIATOWSKI
Singer	Pavarotti	Krzysztof KRAWCZYK
Film Star	Arnold Schwarzenegger	Cezary Pazura
Sportsperson	Alan Shearer	Korzeniowski
painter		ROBERT Jan Matejko
dancer		Aneta Piotr...
TV star		KRZ...
footballer	David Beckham	Jerzy Dudek
detective	Sherlock Holmes	

52 Read and complete the sentences.

1 ......**Sam**............ is tall. He's fair and he's got curly hair. He's got a beard. He hasn't got glasses.

2 ......**Billy**............ is short. He's dark and he's got a moustache. He's got glasses.

3 ......**Tim**............ is tall. He's fair and he's got straight hair. He's got a moustache. He hasn't got glasses.

4 ......**Pat**............ is ......**short**............ . He's ......**dark**...... and he's got a ......**beard**............ . ...**He hasn't got**............ glasses.

Difficult ☐   Quite difficult ☐   OK ☐   Quite easy ☐   Easy ☑

5 Dungeons and Dragons

53

Listen and write the numbers.

(2) princess   (6) dungeon   (1) castle

(4) tower   (5) prince   ( ) dragon

Don't touch the paintings!

1. Welcome to Redhill Castle. Enjoy your visit.
Thank you.

2. OK, everyone, don't run, don't shout and don't touch the paintings!

3. I'm King Speedy having dinner in my castle!
Speedy, get up! Don't sit on the furniture!

4. Come on, follow me!
No, Speedy, don't go that way!

5. Speedy …
Aagh!!!

6. Oh no! It's a secret door. Help!!

7. Mr Crumble?
That's funny! Where is he?

Listen and draw how Mr Crumble gets out of the dungeon.

55

page 90

56

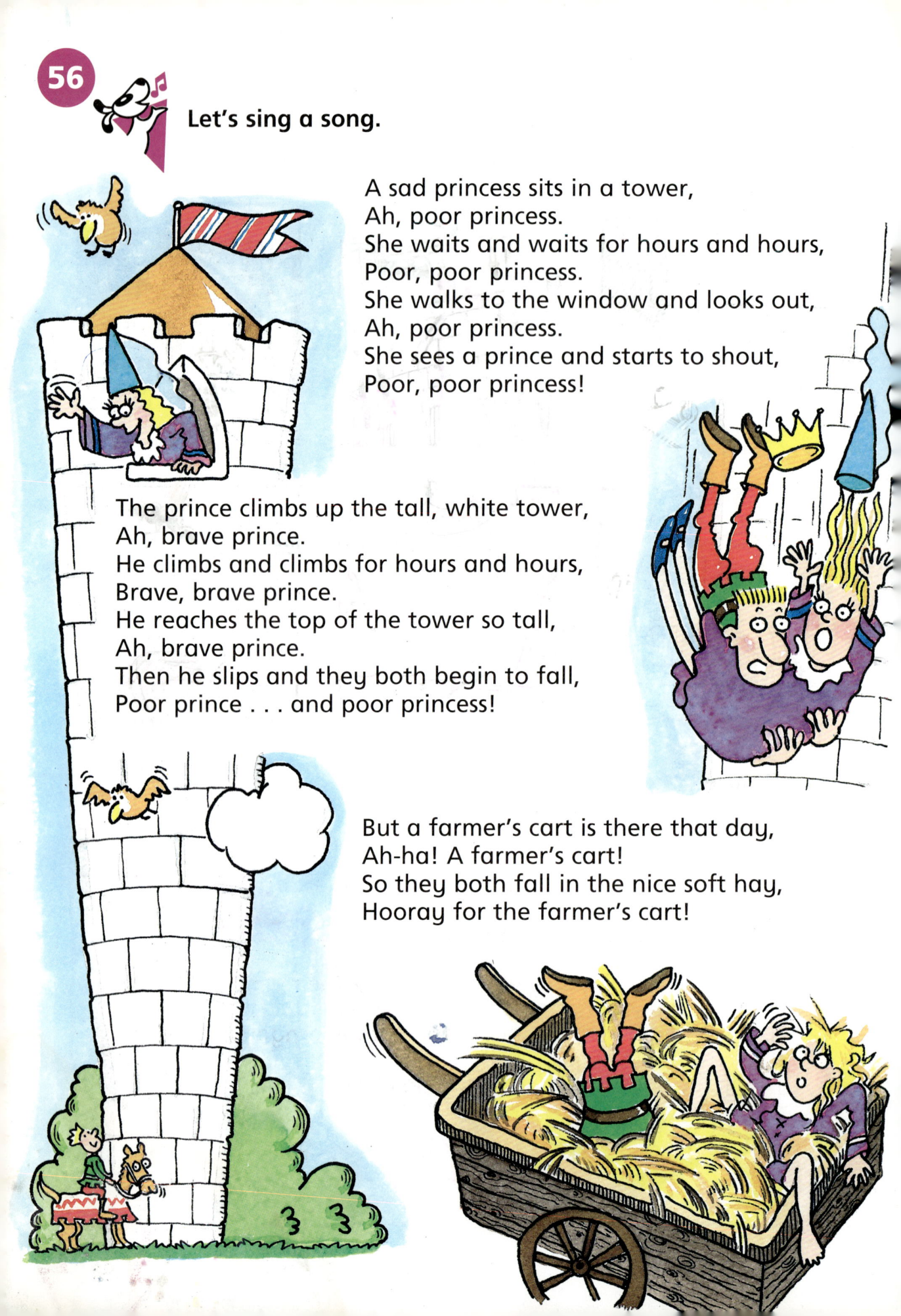

Let's sing a song.

A sad princess sits in a tower,
Ah, poor princess.
She waits and waits for hours and hours,
Poor, poor princess.
She walks to the window and looks out,
Ah, poor princess.
She sees a prince and starts to shout,
Poor, poor princess!

The prince climbs up the tall, white tower,
Ah, brave prince.
He climbs and climbs for hours and hours,
Brave, brave prince.
He reaches the top of the tower so tall,
Ah, brave prince.
Then he slips and they both begin to fall,
Poor prince . . . and poor princess!

But a farmer's cart is there that day,
Ah-ha! A farmer's cart!
So they both fall in the nice soft hay,
Hooray for the farmer's cart!

Princess Harriet is a prisoner! Can she escape?
Read and number.

Picture

☐ Princess Harriet sees a knife.

4 Princess Harriet runs down the stairs.

☐ Princess Harriet is safe!

5 Princess Harriet swims across the river.

1 Princess Harriet waits until the dragon is asleep.

☐ Princess Harriet cuts the rope.

Prince Caspar

Cast
Prince Caspar
Uncle
Servants
Lords and Ladies
Laura
Alice
Friends

Scene 1 In the castle

It's Prince Caspar's birthday today. Everyone is getting ready for his party ... except Prince Caspar's uncle. He's a magician. He's working.

Uncle: Oh, hello Caspar. What time's the party?
Caspar: Eight o'clock. What are you doing?
Uncle: I'm making a magic box ...

Caspar picks up the box and starts to open it.

Uncle: No, Caspar. Don't open it!

The box is open. Strange music plays.

Caspar: I like the music ... but ... I feel ... sleepy...
Servants, Lords and Ladies: We feel sleepy too.

They all go to sleep.

Uncle: It's a magic box ... Give it to ... me ...

He goes to sleep. The music is playing.

...and the Magic Box

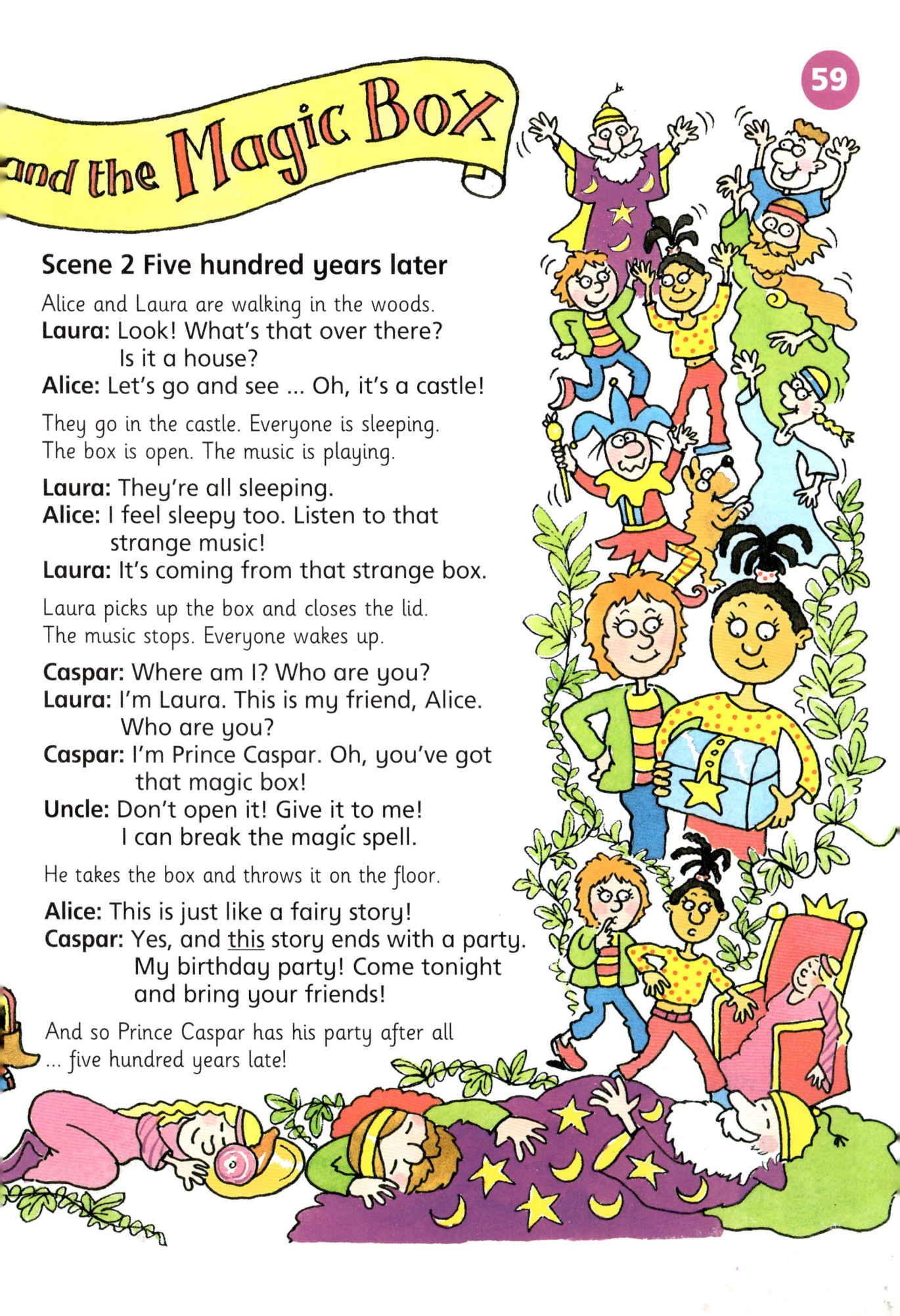

Scene 2 Five hundred years later

Alice and Laura are walking in the woods.
Laura: Look! What's that over there? Is it a house?
Alice: Let's go and see ... Oh, it's a castle!

They go in the castle. Everyone is sleeping. The box is open. The music is playing.

Laura: They're all sleeping.
Alice: I feel sleepy too. Listen to that strange music!
Laura: It's coming from that strange box.

Laura picks up the box and closes the lid. The music stops. Everyone wakes up.

Caspar: Where am I? Who are you?
Laura: I'm Laura. This is my friend, Alice. Who are you?
Caspar: I'm Prince Caspar. Oh, you've got that magic box!
Uncle: Don't open it! Give it to me! I can break the magic spell.

He takes the box and throws it on the floor.

Alice: This is just like a fairy story!
Caspar: Yes, and <u>this</u> story ends with a party. My birthday party! Come tonight and bring your friends!

And so Prince Caspar has his party after all ... five hundred years late!

EPISODE 5
ESCAPE FROM DIAMOND CAVE

1. "Hands up!" "Don't shoot!"

2. "Who are you? What are you doing here?" "We're lost."

3. "I don't believe you. You're trying to steal my diamonds." "No, we aren't. Really. We want to go home …"

4. "Silence! Guards, take them to the castle!" "Ow! Let go! You're hurting me."

5. "Take these spies to the dungeon." "But we aren't spies!"

6. Later … "Don't worry. I know we can escape."

7
What's that ?
There's someone outside the window.
8
Look! It's Glop. Perhaps he can help us to escape.
GLOP
9
What's he doing?
I don't know.
10
CRUNCH!
11
Someone's coming.
Quick!
12
Where are we going?
Don't worry. Follow Glop!

Continues ...

Penfriends

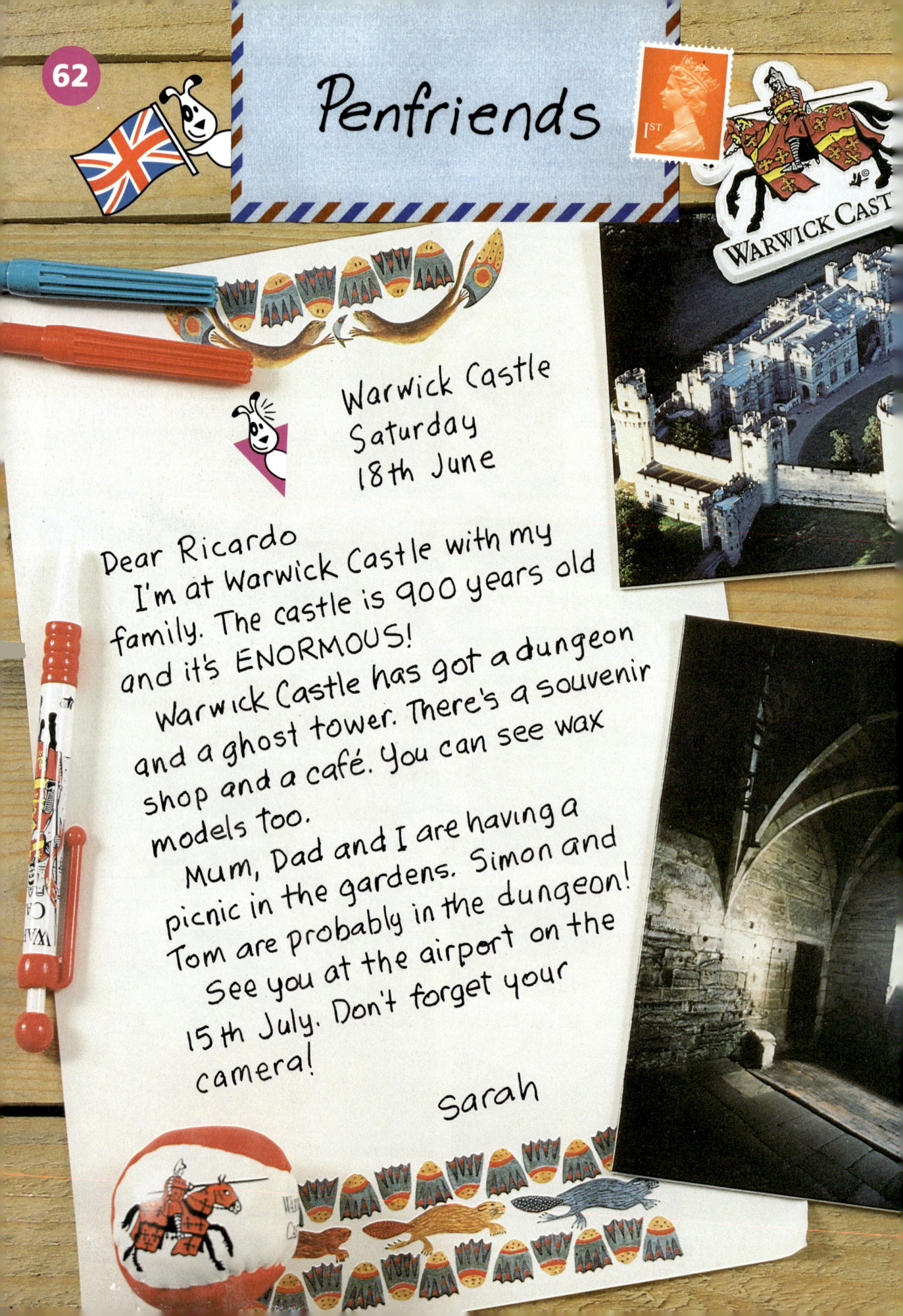

Warwick Castle
Saturday
18th June

Dear Ricardo

I'm at Warwick Castle with my family. The castle is 900 years old and it's ENORMOUS!

Warwick Castle has got a dungeon and a ghost tower. There's a souvenir shop and a café. You can see wax models too.

Mum, Dad and I are having a picnic in the gardens. Simon and Tom are probably in the dungeon!

See you at the airport on the 15th July. Don't forget your camera!

Sarah

63

A Special Place

Where is it?	In Britain	In
What is it?	Warwick Castle	
How old is it?		
What has it got?	a dungeon	
	a gh__t t_w__	
	w__ m_d__s	
	a c__é	
	g__d__s	

64

Listen and number.

Now match to make sentences.

1 He opens   for more food.

2 He asks   down the stairs.

3 She swims   the box.

4 She runs   across the river.

Difficult ☐   Quite difficult ☐   OK ☐   Quite easy ☐   Easy ☐

6 Summer Holidays

Listen and write the numbers.

- ⑥ Italy
- ④ France
- ⑤ Spain
- ① Ireland
- ③ Germany
- ② Britain

Happy Holidays!

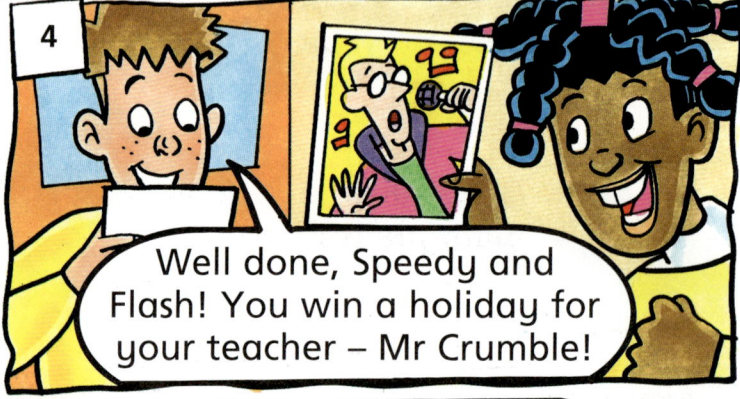

1. Hey, look, Flash! WIN A HOLIDAY FOR YOUR TEACHER. SEND US A FUNNY PHOTO OF YOUR TEACHER AND WIN A HOLIDAY IN ITALY! That's a good idea!

2. Later ... Where's that photo?

3. NEXT WEEK. We've got a letter! Quick, open the envelope.

4. Well done, Speedy and Flash! You win a holiday for your teacher – Mr Crumble!

5. THE LAST DAY OF TERM. Well, goodbye, everyone. Have a nice summer holiday.

6. Where are you going on holiday, Mr Crumble? Oh, nowhere. I'm staying at home.

7. No, you're not. You're going to ITALY! Three cheers for Mr Crumble! Hip, Hip, Hooray!

8. Thanks, everyone!

Listen to Speedy and Flash.

Where are you going on holiday, Speedy?

Spain.

When are you going?

The 13th August.

Now read and choose a holiday. Then write the dialogue and act it out.

RIDE A BIKE IN IRELAND — 29TH JUNE

THE CASTLES OF GERMANY — 3RD JULY

HOTEL IN FRANCE — 1ST SEPTEMBER

BEAUTIFUL BRITAIN — 22ND JULY

CHRISTMAS ON THE BEACH! AUSTRALIA — 19TH DECEMBER

RIDE A HORSE IN THE USA — 14TH SEPTEMBER

Where .... ?

....

When .... ?

....

68

Let's sing a song.

We're all going on a summer holiday,
No more working for a week or two,
Fun and laughter on our summer holiday,
No more worries for me or you.
For a week or two.

We're going where the sun shines brightly,
We're going where the sea is blue,
We've seen it in the movies,
Now let's see if it's true!

Everybody has a summer holiday,
Doing things they always wanted to,
So we're going on a summer holiday,
To make our dreams come true!
For me and you.
For me and you.

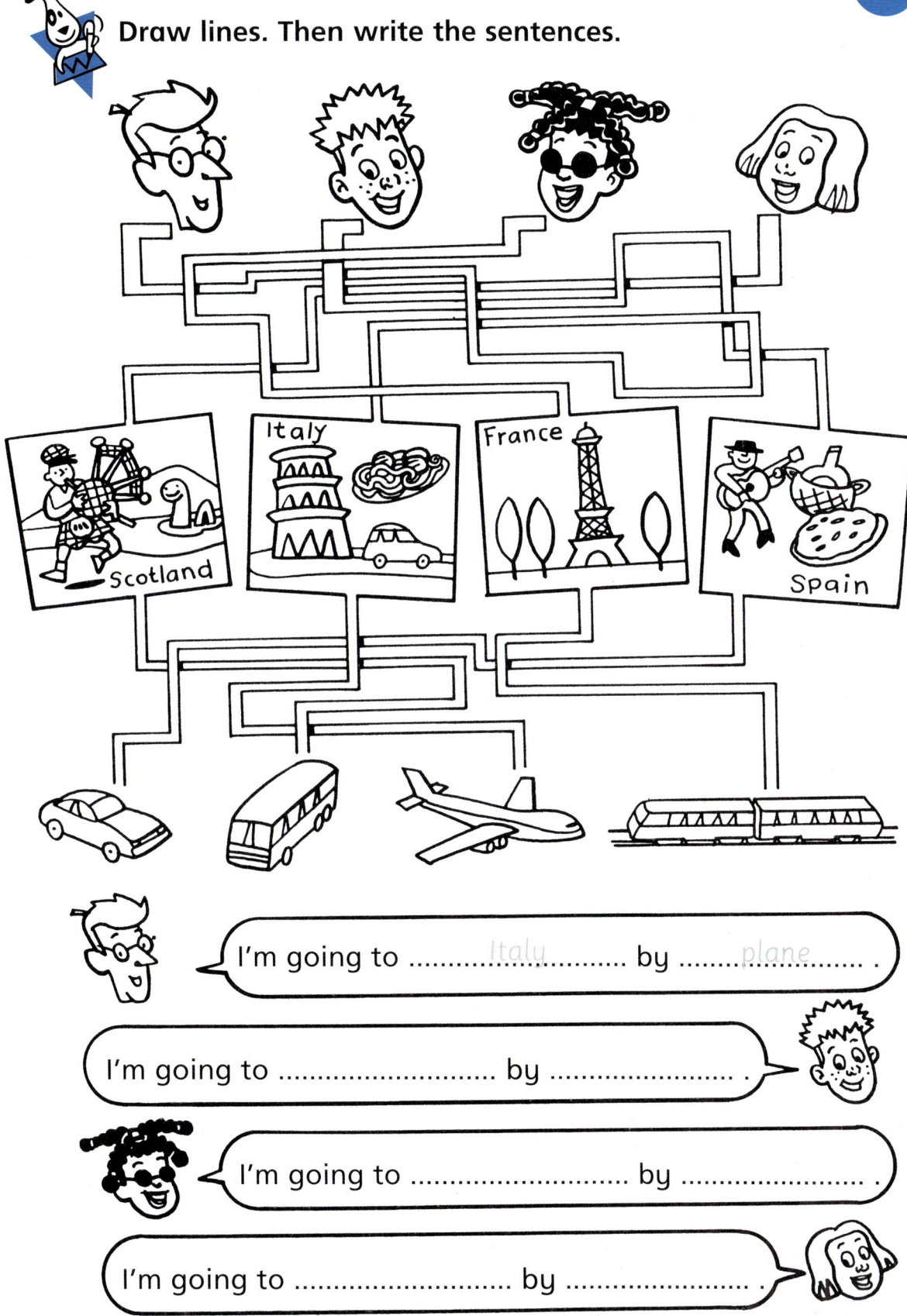

Draw lines. Then write the sentences.

I'm going to ......Italy...... by ......plane...... .

I'm going to .... by ....

I'm going to .... by ....

I'm going to .... by ....

Let's say a chant.

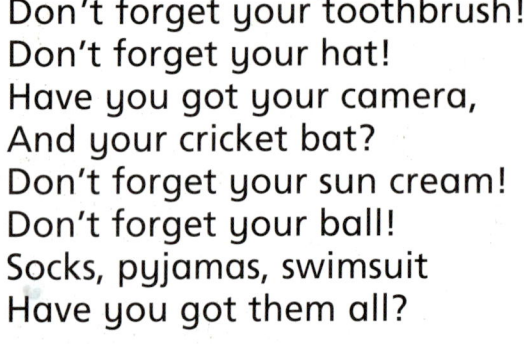

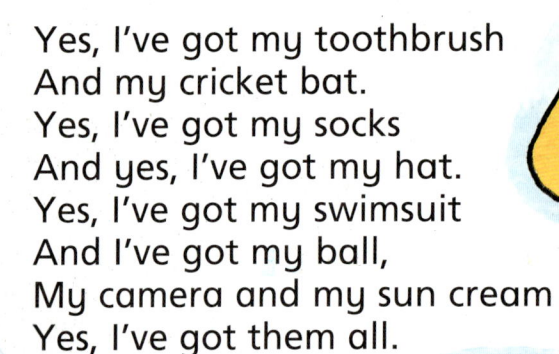

Don't forget your toothbrush!
Don't forget your hat!
Have you got your camera,
And your cricket bat?
Don't forget your sun cream!
Don't forget your ball!
Socks, pyjamas, swimsuit
Have you got them all?

Yes, I've got my toothbrush
And my cricket bat.
Yes, I've got my socks
And yes, I've got my hat.
Yes, I've got my swimsuit
And I've got my ball,
My camera and my sun cream
Yes, I've got them all.

Listen. Then play the game with a friend.

Have you got a camera?
No, I haven't.
Have you got sunglasses?
Yes, I have.
Have you got a hat?
Yes, I have.
Have you got a mask?
No, I haven't.
You're going to Britain!

EPISODE 6
ESCAPE FROM DIAMOND CAVE

1. They're escaping. Close the drawbridge! Stop them!

2. Quick, Mike! Jump!
Hey, you! Stop!

3. Glop and his friends are safe.
Yes, but we aren't. Run!

4. They're coming.
I can't run very fast.

5. It's raining.
A storm is coming.

6. Follow me, Conrad. Don't get lost!

7. Look out! Conrad!

8. Hold on!

9. Help!!!

10. Where are we? Look! The waterfall! We're safe!

11. Are you OK? I think so. What's this?

12. The diamond!!!

THE END

Penfriends

20th July

Hello Sam!
London is SUPER! We're eating ice-creams in Hyde Park. We're going to go to the Tower of London and Big Ben by bus. We want to feed the pigeons in Trafalgar Square and have a boat trip on the Thames. This evening we are going to see a musical at the theatre.
See you soon.
Sarah and Ricardo

The Tower of London

75

Listen and match. Then complete the sentences.

I'm going to ....
by ....
on the ....
....

12TH AUGUST

I'm going to ....
by ....
on the ....
....

30TH SEPTEMBER

I'm going to ....
by ....
on the ....
....

3RD MAY

Difficult ☐   Quite difficult ☐   OK ☐   Quite easy ☐   Easy ☐

Sing a Christmas Carol

Jingle bells, jingle bells,
Jingle all the way!
Oh what fun it is to ride,
In a one horse open sleigh!

Jingle bells, jingle bells,
Jingle all the way!
Oh what fun it is to ride,
In a one horse open sleigh!

April Fool's Day

To play a trick on your friends you need:

a small pencil or pen

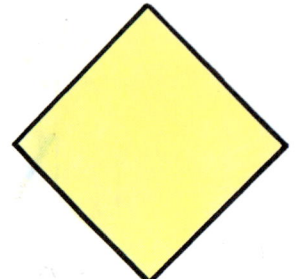

a piece of paper

an audience

1 Put the pencil on the paper.

2 Fold the paper.

3 Roll the pencil up in the paper.

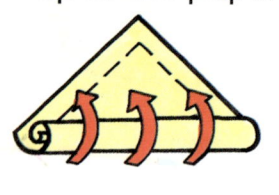

4 Stop when you see both corners.

5 Hold down the bigger corner with one hand.

6 Pull the other corner towards you with the other hand.

7 Where's the pencil? Ha, ha! April Fools!

A May Day Dance

First couple separate,
Go out and round the ring.
Pass your partner going out,
And pass her coming in.
Dance with your partner,
Swing her round and round.
I want to be near you,
You're the one, the one, the one.
I want to be near you,
You're the one for me!

1 Find a partner.

2 Stand in a ring.

3 Skip round the ring.

4 Stand in the ring and face your partner.

5 Swing your partner round and round.

80

Write the letters. Follow the instructions.

a	b	c	d	e	f	g	h	i	j	k	l	m	n	o	p	q	r	s	t	u	v	w	x	y	z

1. colour the ball yellow.

2. draw a dog under the tree.

3. colour the pencil-case green.

4. draw an apple on the table.

Look at the pictures. Write in the speech bubbles.

What time is it?   I've got six.

When's your birthday?   It's on the chair.

How many computer games have you got?   It's ten o'clock.

Where's my English book?   It's in August.

1. How many computer games have you got? — I've got six.

2. Where's my Englisch book? — It's on the chair.

3. When's your birthday? — It's in August

4. What time is it? — It's ten o'clock.

Match the times.

a 1:00   1 It's half past four.

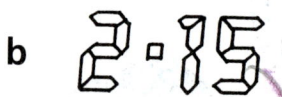

b 2:15   2 It's twenty to three.

c 2:40   3 It's one o'clock.

d 4:30   4 It's twenty past three.

e 3:20   5 It's a quarter to six.

f 5:45   6 It's a quarter past two.

Play bingo.

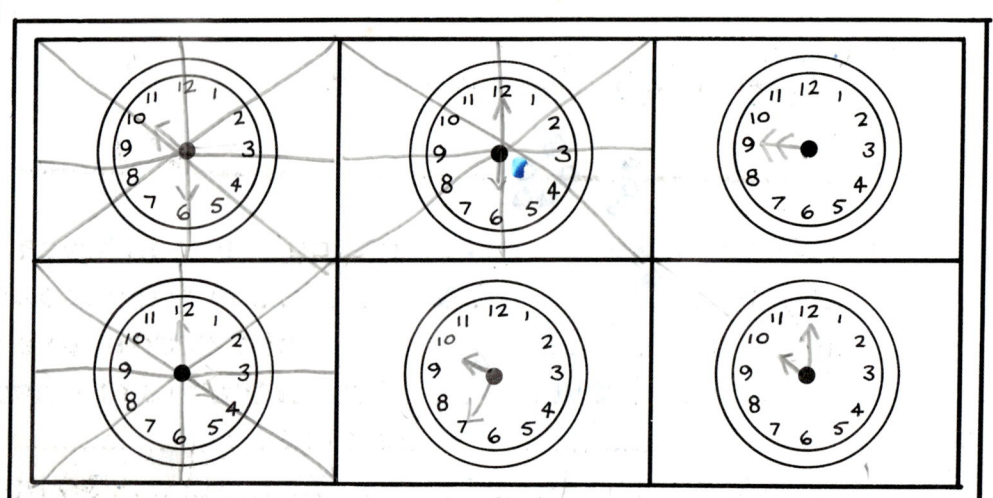

Draw lines to find the times.

Now write about Flash's day.

On school days I ...get up... at a quarter past seven.
Then at ...twenty past seven... I have a shower.
I have my ...breakfast... at a quarter to eight.
At ...ten past eight... I catch the bus to school.
I ...eat half past twelve... lunch at ....
And at a quarter to ...four... I go home.

84

Listen. Write a tick (✓) or a cross (✗).

	🎤	🏊	🎾	🐎	🐐
(boy)	✗	✓	✓	✗	✓
(girl curly)	✗	✓	✗	✗	✓
(girl blonde)	✗	✗	✓	✓	✗
(man)	✓	✗	✗	✗	✓

Now write sentences.

1 Speedy can ...swim, play tenis... and ...chen............ but he can't ...sing............ or ...ride a horse............ .

2 Flash can ...swim............ and ...chen... but he can't ...sing, play......tenis. or ...ride a horse............ .

3 Sally can ...play......tenis... and ...ride a horse...... but he can't ...sing, swim,......... or ...chen............ .

4 Mr Crumble can ...sing,............ and ...chen............ but he can't ...swim, play......tenis.. or ...ride a horse............ .

Unjumble the letters. Write the days.

1 UTHSRYDA — THURSDAY
2 TRSUAAYD — SATURDAY
3 YDUATES — TUESDAY
4 DYMNOA — MONDAY
5 RFYDIA — FRIDAY
6 SWEENDDAY — WEDNESDAY
7 NUDSAY — SUNDAY

Read and complete the diary.

> My favourite day is Saturday. I play football in the morning and go to the cinema in the afternoon. On Mondays and Wednesdays I have my piano lesson. I do my homework on Tuesdays and Thursdays. I watch television on Fridays, and on Sundays I go swimming.

Monday piano lesson	**Friday** television
Tuesday homework	**Saturday** football cinema
Wednesday piano lesson	**Sunday** swimming
Thursday homework	

Write the dates of your special days.

January

February

March

April

May

June

July

August

September

October

November

December

Write the sentences.

Let's have a picnic.

Let's play in the maize

Let's go to svvavi mark

Let's have a ride on the trian!

Let's go to go-kart trak!

Let's go to haus.

Listen and circle. Then draw.

1

~~man~~/woman

~~tall~~/~~short~~

hair: ~~curly~~/straight

fair/~~dark~~

glasses: yes/~~no~~

moustache: yes/no

2

man/~~woman~~

tall/~~short~~

hair: curly/~~straight~~

~~fair~~/dark

glasses: yes/~~no~~

moustache: yes/~~no~~

Write the missing information.

footballer	Madrid	listening
fish	nineteen	Carlos
playing	chips	peas

This is ..Carlos........ . He's a ..footballer........ .
He's ..19........ and he lives in ..Madryd........ .
He likes ..listening........ to music and ..playing........
the guitar. His favourite food is ..fish........ and
..chips........ and ..peas........ . He's great!

Write about a famous person. Stick a photo or draw here.

This is Cezary Pazura.
He's livers in Poland. He's tall
and slim. He's got short black
straight hair. He looks funny.
He's an actor.

Cezary Pazura

Look at the signs. Write the sentences.

| ~~run~~ | go upstairs | turn left |
| shout | eat ice-cream | climb the trees |

1 Don't run

2 Don't climb the trees.

3 Don't shout.

4 Don't turn left.

5 Don't eat ice-cream

6 Don't go upstairs.

Draw a sign. Write the instruction.

Don't take photos
....
....

Read and write the numbers.

Picture

- [3] She sees a rabbit and she falls down a hole.
- [4] He sees a footprint. He finds a man and calls him Friday.
- [2] He wakes up but he can't stand up! He sees a lot of small people.
- [1] He asks for more food. He runs away and walks to London.

92

Use the key and colour the flags.
Write the names of the countries.

1 blue 2 white 3 red 4 black 5 yellow 6 green 7 orange

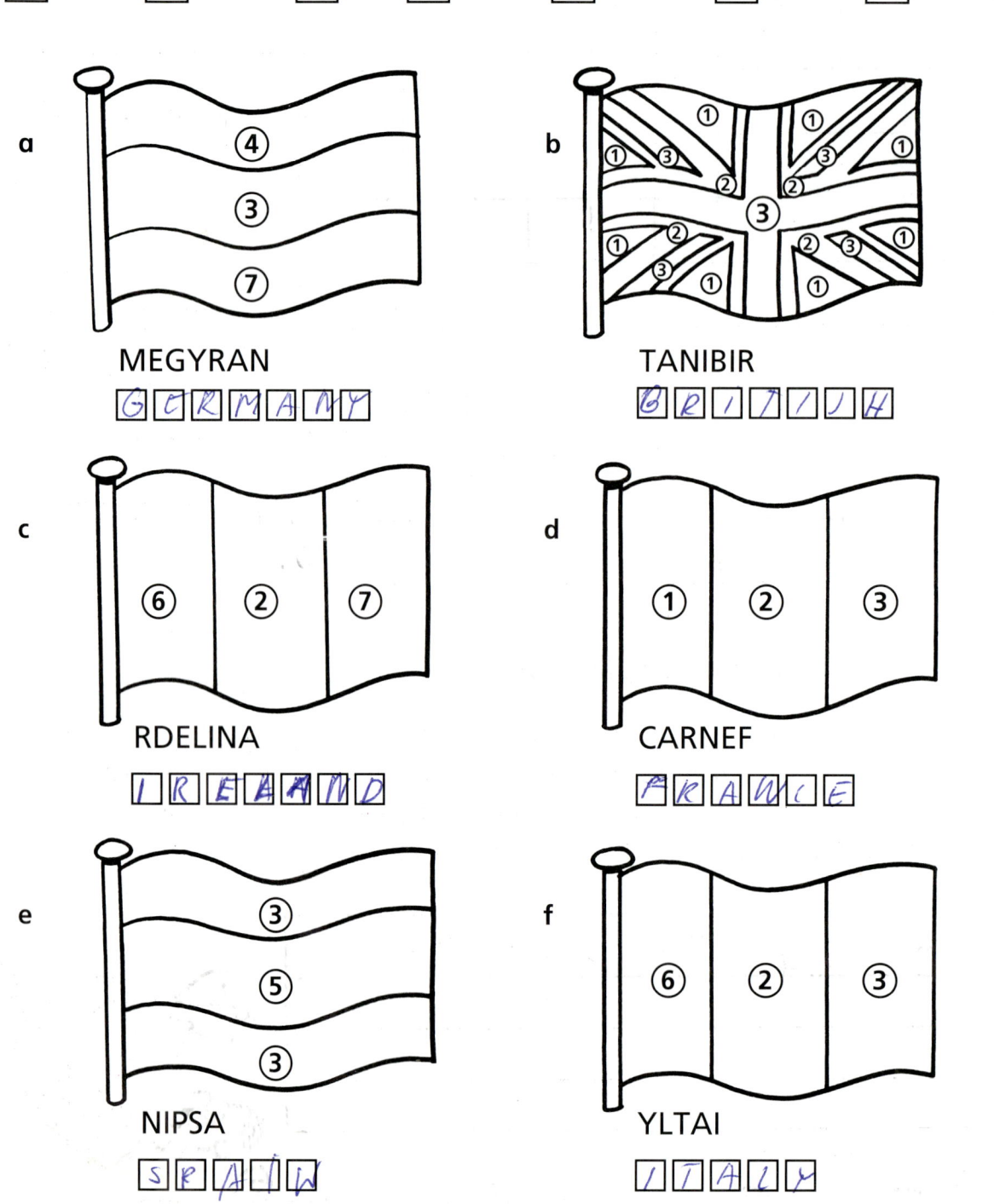

a) MEGYRAN — GERMANY

b) TANIBIR — BRITISH

c) RDELINA — IRELAND

d) CARNEF — FRANCE

e) NIPSA — SPAIN

f) YLTAI — ITALY

Choose ten words from pages 70 and 71 and make a word square. Give it to a friend.

1 ....
2 ....
3 ....
4 ....
5 ....
6 ....
7 ....
8 ....
9 ....
10 ....

Read and complete the table.

Harry, Jack and Laura are friends. They are all going on holiday. The person going by car is going to Spain. Harry is not going to France. Jack is not going by plane. The girl is going to Italy.

Name	Country	Transport

Glossary

In the playground
beginning with	3
What time is it?	4

Unit 1
a pair of ...	13
a quarter past	5
a quarter to	5
brush	8
bye	14
cave	12
cello lessons	14
clean	8
continues	13
diamond	12
Don't be late ...	12
early	6
episode	12
escape	12
get up	9
glasses	12
half past	5
have a bath	9
have dinner	14
have lunch	14
homework	9
I'm going for a walk	12
Monday	8
morning	8
on the other side of	13
penfriends	14
quite	16
soon	14
start	6
stay	8
Sunday	8
Take my hand.	13
Tell me about ...	14
there	13
This is the way I...	8
twelve o'clock	8
twenty past	7
twenty to	6
twenty-five	9
wash	8
waterfall	12
world	14
wrong	6
You idiot!	12

Unit 2
after	26
against	26
alphabet	22
amazing	24
another	26
backwards	23
bakery	20
band	18
basketball	19
beautiful	25
brilliant	18
click your fingers	23
computer screen	20
cook	17
dance	17
daylight	24
drama club	26
drive	20
drums	18
English	22
far	20
French club	26
get in	20
get out	24
guitar	17
in the evenings	20
inside	24
keyboards	18
Look out!	24
magazine	20
match	26
minute	23
netball	26
office block	20
on Friday nights	20
phone	20
photo	26
play	17
ride a bike	19
ride on the waves	20
safe	24
seaside	20
ski	19
someone	19
sometimes	26
spell	23
surfboard	20
swimming club	26
That's great!	18
Thursday	21
tongue	22
touch	22
Tuesday	21
watch	20
Wednesday	21
week	20
What a ...!	25
What's that?	25
whistle	23
work	20

Unit 3
£ symbol for pound sterling	32
a.m.	32
about	32
Another one?	37
bench	35
bin	35
café	34
calendar	38
Come on.	37
date	31
exit	35
footprints	37
fountain	35
free	32
giant	37
go-kart track	32
greedy	37
Happy birthday	30
Have a ride ...	32
Have a special day...	32
hear	40
him	36
I can't remember.	31
invitation	31
invite	31
Keep writing.	38
later	36
Let's go!	37
lion	35
lost	36
maze	32
open	32
out of the maze	35
p.m.	32
people	37
perhaps	36
safari park	32
send	38
statue	35
train	32
understands	36
visit	33
watch	38

Unit 4
a few	49
actor	41
actress	42
all over the world	50
American	46
anywhere	47
athlete	41
beard	43
called	46
chart	46
curly	43
dancer	41
dark	43
down the street	47
drive	47
Edinburgh	46
fair	43
famous	41
fellow	47
footballer	41
full of	50
handsome	47
He's really cool!	46
he/she takes	46
he/she travels	46
help	48
how	48
interesting	47
Is she wearing ...?	42
It's hot ...	48
job	46
king	50
London	50
moustache	44
museum	50
name the star	45
never	47
nineteen	46
on TV	42
Paris	46
policewoman	50
poor things	48
queen	50
queue	50
ready	49
Scottish	46
sensational	47
sentences	52
she/he lives in ...	46
short	43
shy	47
singer	41
straight	43
sun tan	47
tall	43
thanks	42
that's	43
them	48
There she is ...	42
There's ...!	42
tired	48
twenty eight	46
voices	48
Watch out for ...	49
wax models	50
What's happening?	49
wherever	47

wives	50

Unit 5

across	57
airport	62
asleep	57
both	56
box	58
bring	59
camera	62
cart	56
castle	53
closes	59
dinner	54
don't	54
dragon	53
dungeon	53
ends	59
enjoy	54
enormous	62
everyone	54
except	58
forget	62
get ready	58
Give it to me.	58
go to sleep	58
guard	60
Hands up!	60
hay	56
he/she reaches	56
he/she slips	56
hour	56
hundred	59
I can break the magic spell	59
I don't believe you.	60
I feel sleepy.	58
I'm making	58
knife	57
Let go!	60
lid	59
magician	58
No, we aren't.	60
Oh, dear!	55
open	58
outside	61
paintings	54
prince	53
princess	53
prisoner	57
probably	62
really	60
rope	57
sad	56
secret	54
See you...	62
shoot	60
shout	54
silence	60
so	56
soft	56
spies	60
stairs	57
start	55
strange	58
take them	60
that way	54
That's funny!	54
This is just like a fairy story.	59
tonight	59
top	56
tower	53
uncle	58
until	57
wakes up	59
waits	56
woods	59
worry: don't worry	61
You're hurting me.	60
You're trying to steal ...	60

Unit 6

bat (cricket)	70
boat trip	74
Britain	65
by (plane)	69
choose	67
Doing things they always wanted to	68
Don't get lost!	72
drawbridge	72
end	73
envelope	66
feed	74
forget	70
France	65
Germany	65
Hold on!	73
holiday	65
I think so.	73
Ireland	65
It's raining.	72
Italy	65
laughter	68
mask	71
musical	74
next week	66
nowhere	66
pigeons	74
safe	72
Scotland	69
sea	68
send us	66
shines brightly	68
Spain	65
stay at home	66
storm	72
summer	65
sun cream	70
sunglasses	71
super	74
swimsuit	70
the last day of term	66
theatre	74
Three cheers for ...	66
To make our dreams come true	68
toothbrush	70
We've seen it in the movies	68
Well done!	66
win	66
worries	68

Supplementary activities

all the way	77
April's Fool Day	78
audience	78
Christmas Carol	77
coming in	79
couple	79
face	79
going out	79
her	79
I want to be near you.	79
jingle	77
May Day	79
near	79
paper	78
partner	79
pass	79
piece	78
play a trick	78
ring	78
roll up	78
round the ...	79
separate	79
sleigh	77
swing around	79
towards	78
You're the one for me.	79

Reinforcement activities

countries	92
falls down	91
flag	92
hole	91
key	92
Let's have a picnic.	87
person	93
runs away	91
speech bubble	81
unjumble	85
woman	88

OXFORD
UNIVERSITY PRESS

Great Clarendon Street, Oxford OX2 6DP

Oxford University Press is a department of the University of Oxford.
It furthers the University's objective of excellence in research, scholarship,
and education by publishing worldwide in

Oxford New York

Auckland Cape Town Dar es Salaam Hong Kong Karachi
Kuala Lumpur Madrid Melbourne Mexico City Nairobi
New Delhi Shanghai Taipei Toronto

With offices in

Argentina Austria Brazil Chile Czech Republic France Greece
Guatemala Hungary Italy Japan Poland Portugal Singapore
South Korea Switzerland Thailand Turkey Ukraine Vietnam

OXFORD and OXFORD ENGLISH are registered trade marks of
Oxford University Press in the UK and in certain other countries

© Oxford University Press 1997

The moral rights of the author have been asserted

Database right Oxford University Press (maker)

First published in this edition 1998
2009 2008 2007 2006 2005
10 9 8 7 6 5

No unauthorized photocopying

All rights reserved. No part of this publication may be reproduced,
stored in a retrieval system, or transmitted, in any form or by any
means, without the prior permission in writing of Oxford University
Press, or as expressly permitted by law, or under terms agreed with the
appropriate reprographics rights organization. Enquiries concerning
reproduction outside the scope of the above should be sent to the
ELT Rights Department, Oxford University Press, at the address above

You must not circulate this book in any other binding or cover
and you must impose this same condition on any acquirer

Any websites referred to in this publication are in the public domain
and their addresses are provided by Oxford University Press for
information only. Oxford University Press disclaims any responsibility
for the content

ISBN-13: 978 0 19 432040 5
ISBN-10: 0 19 432040 5

Printed in China

ACKNOWLEDGEMENTS

*The publishers would like to thank the following for their much valued
assistance:* Artists' Collective Theatre School; The Hampshire
Schools – London; Madame Tussaud's; Warwick Castle

"Escape from Diamond Cave" is by Paul Davies

Illustrations by: John Haslam, Lorna Kent, Chris Smedley

Location photography by: Lesley Howling

Studio photography by: Julie Fisher